MASTERS of INVENTION

EDWIN LAND

Photographic Pioneer

Scott McPartland

ROURKE ENTERPRISES,INC.
VERO BEACH, FLORIDA 32964

© 1993 Rourke Enterprises, Inc.

A Blackbirch Graphics book.

Library of Congress Cataloging-in-Publication Data

McPartland, Scott, 1952–
    Edwin Land / by Scott McPartland.
       p.   cm. — (Masters of invention)
    Includes index.
    Summary: A biography of the scientist whose many inventions include the Polaroid camera.
    ISBN 0-86592-150-4
    1. Land, Edwin Herbert, 1909–1991—Juvenile literature. 2. Polaroid Land camera—History—Juvenile literature. [1. Land, Edwin Herbert, 1909–1991. 2. Scientists. 3. Inventors. 4. Polaroid Land camera.] I. Title. II. Series.
TR540.L36M37   1993
681'.418'092—dc20
[B]   93-22077
                                                CIP
                                              AC

CONTENTS

GENIUS IN THE MAKING

*Edwin showed his willingness to do things his
own way, no matter what others thought.*

*M*any times scientists and inventors exaggerate their stories to make it appear as if they are much more brilliant and inspired than the rest of us. We often get the impression that great scientists were geniuses from childhood and that they never had to struggle with failure like the rest of us.

Edwin Land, the man who created the Polaroid camera, the first instant camera, seems like just such a person. The light of his genius shined almost continually from his early years until his death in 1991. Edwin will be remembered for his world-famous camera, but he is also the inventor of dozens of other important products. He holds more than 530 patents, second only to Thomas Edison. He was the

Opposite: Although he is best known for having invented the instant camera, Edwin Land holds over 530 patents—second only to Thomas Edison. He will undoubtedly be remembered as one of the greatest scientists of the twentieth century.

founder of one of America's most successful companies. Among scientists, he is considered a unique individual and an original thinker.

If we look closely at his life, however, we see that his story was really about hard work and unending dedication. Edwin's success comes as much from his character as from his genius. Even when he failed, he remained true to his ideals. Many people in business believe that success is measured by wealth, but to Edwin Land, "the bottom line is in heaven."

A Young Photographer

Edwin was born in Bridgeport, Connecticut, on May 7, 1909, the only child of Harry and Martha Land. His father was a wealthy land-owner and a scrap and iron dealer. As a young boy, Edwin pronounced his name "Din," and this is what his family and close friends called him throughout his life.

The Land family moved from Bridgeport to Norwich, Connecticut, where Edwin attended Norwich Academy. It was there that teachers first began to notice his genius.

Edwin was interested in photography at an early age. The first picture he developed was of his family's poodle. The dog would often run away, so when Edwin finally lost his dog, he was comforted by the photograph. He described taking and keeping the picture as

As a child, Edwin used to enjoy taking pictures of his dog at his family home in Norwich, Connecticut.

a way of making something that was both "outside himself and part of himself."

Edwin was not simply interested in taking pictures as a hobby. He was curious about how photographs were created. He began to read about optics, the study of vision and light.

Edwin's interest in optics later turned out to be the basis for his scientific contribution.

An Outstanding Student

Edwin read everything he could about physics, especially about light and optics. One of the books that influenced him most was R.W. Wood's *Physical Optics*. Edwin also developed an interest in the work of Michael Faraday, the great English scientist who made original discoveries in optics, electricity, and chemistry.

When he was 12, Edwin attended summer camp in New York. There he became friends with one of the counselors, Julius Silver, who was also interested in science. Together, Julius and Edwin were able to rewire the entire camp, a remarkable feat for two young boys.

At Norwich, Edwin was on the school's track and debating teams. He achieved an excellent academic record, too. Edwin did so well that he graduated from Norwich at only 16 and was accepted at Harvard University, one of America's best schools.

A "Bright" Idea

During his first year at Harvard, Edwin took a trip to New York City. As he was walking around the Broadway theater area, Edwin was impressed by all the huge, brightly lit signs. The glare from these signs was intense. It was almost like looking into the sun.

Edwin wondered whether there wasn't a better way to make these signs so there would be less glare. From this casual observation, Edwin began to think about the problem of normal electric lights in an original way.

Soon he had an idea to use polarizers to cut down on the glare. The properties of polarizers were known since Faraday's time.

In fact, Faraday himself had experimented on an important polarizer, a rock crystal called Iceland spar. Shining a light through spar crystal revealed that the tight structure of the molecules allowed traveling light rays to pass through in one direction only. This made the light more focused.

Scientists soon realized that crystals could be used to make light more organized. The problem was that rock crystal is very heavy and expensive. Certain kinds of glass lenses, called Fresnel lenses were used in lighthouses and for stage lights. These lenses were not only heavy and expensive, but they were also quite fragile.

Edwin's problem was finding a lightweight, durable material that could polarize light and that could also be made at a reasonable cost. At first Edwin thought it would be easy. He believed that within a few months he'd find the answer.

An Independent Spirit

Edwin dropped out of Harvard and moved to New York City. Some people thought it odd that Edwin would leave college and go off on his own. But the young inventor didn't seem to care. This was the first time Edwin showed his willingness to do things his own way, no matter what others thought.

GETTING DOWN TO BUSINESS

Edwin faced repeated setbacks, but he never surrendered his commitment.

*W*hen Edwin first moved to New York City, he lived in a small apartment on 55th Street. His apartment was not too far from the theater district that had originally inspired his idea. During the day, Edwin went to the New York Public Library on Fifth Avenue, the only library in the country that was bigger than Harvard's. Edwin read everything on the subject of optics.

Experimentation

A scientist needs more than just books to do research. He or she also needs access to a laboratory, a place to carry out experiments. Edwin overcame that problem by going up to

Columbia University at night. One of the windows in the physics lab was usually left open. Edwin had no trouble sneaking in, doing his experiments, and sneaking back out again.

Edwin spent three years in New York City, reading, experimenting, and thinking. The breakthrough that Edwin thought would be short in coming was still years in his future. The time spent alone was valuable, however, because it proved to be the basis of his future success.

When Edwin was living in New York City, he often sneaked into Columbia University's physics laboratory, where he could do his experiments.

A Team Is United

Perhaps even more valuable than his work alone was Edwin's meeting with Helen Maislen of Hartford, Connecticut. Helen, who was called Terre by her friends, worked as Edwin's assistant. She and Edwin made such a good team that when Edwin was ready to leave New York, he asked Terre to be his wife. They remained together for the rest of Edwin's life.

Edwin Returns to Harvard

Edwin decided to reapply to Harvard and was immediately welcomed back. There he met George Wheelwright III, an assistant in the physics department who was in charge of the lab where Edwin and Terre worked. Edwin and George worked closely together and quickly became friends.

Three years after returning to Harvard, Edwin perfected his process for creating a polarizing material. He presented a paper titled "A New Polarizer for Light in the Form of an Extensive Synthetic Sheet" that announced his breakthrough. Edwin had come up with a way to create tiny, synthetic, needle-shaped crystals arranged on a plastic sheet in such a way that they transmitted light waves through only one plane of the axis, just as a single, enormous crystal would.

Edwin was just 23 years old. He needed only one more semester at Harvard until he graduated. With his talent for optical physics he would certainly have been given a place in the graduate program. After a year or two of research, he could have received his Ph.D. and spent his life as a professor.

Forming His Own Company

But Edwin didn't want to do things that way. Instead, he dropped out of school again. This time, he never went back. He called his old camp counselor, Julius Silver, who was now a lawyer, and asked him for help patenting the polarizing process. Silver and another lawyer, Donald Brown, started making preparations.

Edwin's first synthetic polarizing sheets were called Polaroid J-sheets. The name *Polaroid* was suggested by Professor Clarence Kennedy of Smith College. The ending *oid* means "like," or "resembling." The word *Polaroid* would later become so common that most people would have trouble remembering a time before it was part of everyday language.

Silver and Brown secured a patent. The safe course for Edwin would have been to license his discovery to a big company in exchange for a royalty or a large cash or stock payment. But Edwin was determined to start his own company.

He wanted to create a place where he was free to pursue the kind of research he wanted to do, research that would benefit people by creating products they could use. Edwin wanted the freedom to pursue the science that interested him and the power to run his own company in the way he thought was right.

Edwin asked George Wheelwright, his former physics instructor, to join him. Even though Edwin thought of his partner as more experienced, he was only two years older than Edwin. With financial help from their parents, they started the Land-Wheelwright Laboratories in a barn in Wellesley, Massachusetts.

At first they did only consulting and some research. But soon, they got their first big job. Kodak, the giant photography company wanted Land-Wheelwright to make light filters out of Edwin's new polarizing plastic.

The company grew. Soon, the company's headquarters moved from the Wellesley barn to a basement in Boston. Land-Wheelwright began hiring additional workers. But in order to survive, the company needed to find other markets for its product.

A New Kind of Sunglasses

It was then that another of Edwin's gifts came out. He invited a number of people from the American Optical Company to a demonstration

American Optical executives saw how well Edwin's polarized sunglasses reduced glare when they looked into a fish tank set up next to a sun-filled window.

of the J-sheets. Edwin took them to a hotel suite. Inside, he had set up a large fish tank near the window to reflect the bright sunlight. The men from American Optical were having trouble avoiding the painful glare. Edwin then handed each of them a pair of his new polarized sunglasses. The glare was instantly gone, and Land-Wheelwright had a new customer.

The American Optical Company began using J-sheets to make "Polaroid Day Glasses." Before that time, sunglasses were usually just blackened lenses that did nothing to protect against glare or direct sunlight. Edwin's revolutionary lenses actually reduced the amount of sun that was let in. They set a new standard for the entire industry.

Determination in the Face of Failure

With customers like Kodak and American Optical, Land-Wheelwright was on its way. But Edwin kept trying to figure out how he could use the J-sheets to improve life. He noticed that the glare from car headlights was a major problem. In the days before brightly lit highways, most Americans drove at night along dark roads. Drivers often lost control of their cars when suddenly faced by the glare of oncoming headlights. Pedestrians were sometimes blinded by cars and unable to get out of the way.

Edwin wrote the words "400 people killed every night" on the blackboard of his laboratory as a reminder of how serious the problem of headlight fatalities was, and he set to work. He said he felt exactly like a doctor working on a cure for a deadly disease.

Within a short time, he developed a way to use Polaroid filters on headlights. Edwin presented his idea to carmakers, fully expecting that they would immediately adopt it. They seemed interested, but they had questions about his product and worried about how well it would work. They wondered, for instance, if the heat produced by the lights would melt the plastic filter.

Edwin went back to the laboratory and improved his product. He developed a K polarizer that could withstand heat and bright

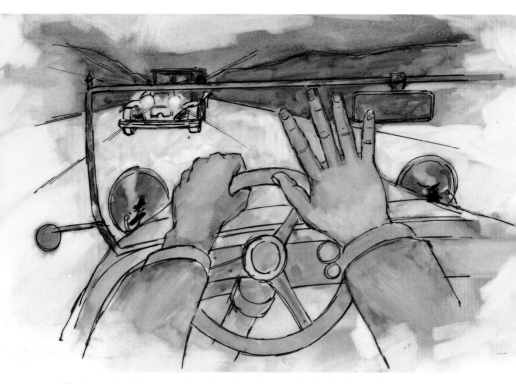

Edwin worked long and hard to develop polarized sheets that would cover car headlights and reduce their dangerous, blinding glare.

light. Again and again, he brought his results to the auto manufacturers in Detroit, Michigan. They were interested but would not commit themselves to buying the product.

Edwin spent years trying to persuade the carmakers in Detroit to use his filters on their headlights, but he never succeeded. At a time when his own company was still struggling to establish itself, he invested time and money that might have been used in other pursuits because he believed strongly in what he was doing. Edwin faced repeated setbacks, but he never surrendered his commitment.

Birth of the Polaroid Corporation

Although Edwin's headlight idea was a failure, a related product was a glare-free filter for desk lamps that made office work easier on the eyes. There seemed to be no end to the new uses for his polarizing sheets.

Land-Wheelwright was attracting attention. Major Wall Street investors were interested in Edwin and his work. His polarizing sheets represented a revolutionary step forward in lighting. But moreover, Edwin's was one of the companies that would help pull the nation out of the Great Depression of the 1930s. The development of new industries would help the nation recover. Investors wanted to help Land-Wheelwright realize its potential.

In 1937, Land-Wheelwright became the Polaroid Corporation. Wall Street investors provided Edwin with a huge sum of money to grow, but they also gave him an enormous amount of freedom to do things the way he wanted. Edwin, Terre, and George controlled a large block of the stock and, along with Julius Silver, made all the major decisions.

The new Polaroid Corporation stayed in Boston, but moved to larger quarters, an old warehouse on Columbus Avenue. Edwin hired more people, including William J. McCune, in 1939. McCune's ability to make almost anything that Land described made him a very valuable worker. The two men began a life-long association, which was crowned by McCune succeeding Land as president of Polaroid in 1975.

Edwin and his team continued to explore new areas for polarizing plastic. Most of the company's money, however, still came from selling the rights to sunglasses and camera lenses. Then, a new and unexpected area opened up for Polaroid when America entered World War II in 1941.

In the lab, Edwin spent much of his time working with colleagues on developing better and stronger polarizers.

Helping the War Effort

Because of Polaroid's experience in optical research, the government granted Edwin and his team contracts to work on ways to improve vision in combat. The company expanded tremendously during the war, but there was also a significant loss. George Wheelwright left Polaroid to become a navigator in the navy air force. Although he survived the war, he never returned to Polaroid. George's place as Edwin's chief assistant was then taken over by William McCune.

Edwin and his team created many new and improved products that helped America win the war. Among these products were bomb-sights, periscopes, plastic lenses that made tank guns safer, goggles that let pilots see at night, and range finders. Polaroid's biggest project, however, was the development of a guidance system that enabled a bomb to be released far away from its target and to head toward the heat given off by a ship's engines. Although the breakthrough came too late to be used during the war, the guidance system became the basis of heat-seeking missiles in use today.

The war also created a major problem for Edwin. One of the materials he used to make his polarizing sheets contained quinine. Quinine is made from the bark of the cinchona

During World War II, Edwin and his team worked tirelessly to create a heat-seeking guidance system that would allow pilots to fire at targets from far away.

tree, which is found only in Java. In 1942, the Japanese, whom the United States was fighting against, captured Java, completely cutting off the world's supply of quinine.

This was a terrible blow, not because of quinine's value to industry, but because it was also the only treatment for malaria. With the U.S. troops fighting a jungle war in the Pacific, thousands would contract malaria from insect bites, and without quinine many would die.

Edwin had already been working to find a different material to use in his polarizing sheets.

By the time Java was captured, he had succeeded. The new L-sheets turned out to be even better than the older materials.

Edwin had solved the problem for his own company, but, typically, he did not stop there. He hired the best chemists he could find and began working with them on a substitute for quinine that could be used against malaria. A little more than a year later, they developed a formula for synthetic quinine, which they gave to the government for free.

Another war project turned out to be the most important of all for Edwin. The government asked Polaroid to devise a new kind of aerial camera that could take three-dimensional pictures of target sights. This would help U.S. pilots see the land below more accurately. As usual, Edwin studied extensively, reading everything he could on the subject of photography, until he thoroughly understood the physics and chemistry behind taking pictures.

In time, Edwin and his team came up with a way to run two projectors together, and they developed special glasses that gave the illusion of depth to the overlapping images. They also began working on new kinds of color film. Edwin hoped that when the war ended he could develop these projects into new forms of entertainment. At this point, Edwin didn't realize how much time he would spend working with photography.

THE FIRST INSTANT CAMERA

*"If you are able to state a problem...then
that problem can be solved."*

*L*ate in 1943, Edwin and his family took a short vacation to Santa Fe, New Mexico. One day, Edwin and his three-year-old daughter Jeffie were sightseeing and taking pictures. Jeffie was excited to see how the pictures would come out. Edwin explained that there was no way to see the pictures right away.

Edwin's Daughter Sparks an Idea

Jeffie didn't understand. "Why can't I see it now?" she asked. All of the work Edwin had done on aerial cameras and new kinds of film suddenly came together in his mind as he thought of a way to answer his daughter. Why couldn't someone build a camera that instantly developed its own film?

23

While having her picture taken, Edwin's daughter asked why it had to take so long for the film to be developed. This was all the inspiration Edwin needed—soon he was fast at work developing his Polaroid instant camera.

Developing a photograph is a complicated process. A camera is really just a dark box that lets a controlled amount of light onto a tiny piece of plastic film treated with light-sensitive chemicals called silver halides. The areas of film that are exposed react most.

Most film has to be carefully taken out of the camera in a dark place because it will still react to any light. Then the film is placed in a pan of developing solution. The solution turns the silver halides into metallic silver, making the parts of the film exposed to the most light turn the blackest. This is why the first step in developing film is called producing a negative—the light areas become dark, exactly the opposite of how the scene looked in real life.

Next, the negative is soaked in another solution so it will no longer react to light. This is called fixing. It is washed to remove excess chemicals and once it is dry, the negative can be turned into a positive by repeating the process. This time, light-sensitive paper is exposed under the negative. This paper, also called a positive, is what a photograph really is.

Edwin's daughter was asking him why all these steps couldn't be done at the same time without pans or drying or waiting. Most other fathers would have said, "Because they can't." But Edwin Land wasn't like most fathers.

Whenever his research team was stuck on a problem and didn't know what to do next, Edwin would tell them that the most important part of scientific discovery wasn't a question of having more information, but of asking the right questions. "If you are able to state a problem...then that problem can be solved," he said. All they needed to do was to think about the problem in a new way—to ask better questions—and the solution would come.

He wandered around Sante Fe, thinking. He later said, "All that we at Polaroid had learned about making polarizers and plastics, and the properties of viscous [sticky] liquids, and the preparation of microscopic crystals smaller than the wavelengths of light was preparation for that day in which I suddenly knew how to make a one-step photographic process."

All at once, a lifetime of study and experimentation came together in a moment of clarity and power. Edwin saw in his mind a camera that would instantly develop a positive picture without pans of chemicals. He didn't exactly know how each step would work. He was just thinking in images and pictures, just getting the concept clear in his mind.

A Secret Project

He went to where his friend Donald Brown was staying in Sante Fe and excitedly began to describe his ideas. Even though Donald was not a scientist, he and Edwin stayed up half the night making notes and drawing plans. The next morning, Edwin called his lab. He told the crew to begin a new secret-project file, number SX-70, and start research immediately.

At the time, most of the company, including Edwin himself and William McCune, were still working on another top-secret project—to make heat-seeking bombs. No matter how exciting the possibility of instant photography was, there was still a war to win.

Edwin himself came up with the major technical elements of the new camera. A "pod" of chemical jelly would burst open when film went through precisely timed rollers. The rollers would sandwich positive and negative sheets, on which a picture would develop.

Most of the actual early experiments, however, were carried out by Doxie Muller, Maxfield Parrish, and Fred Binda. Edwin reviewed their progress and sometimes offered suggestions, but it was their job to work out the details.

With the end of World War II in the summer of 1945, the services of Polaroid were no longer in demand by the U.S. government. As a result, Edwin had to let many good workers go. Realizing that he could not forever rely on government contracts, which were dependent on world events, he decided to transfer all his attention to his new camera.

Edwin was staking a lot on the camera's success. There were still technical problems to work out. Although Edwin was sure that he and his staff would overcome the difficulties, he still worried that no one would buy the camera. Edwin never stopped having faith in his vision, and he forged ahead.

By early 1946, Polaroid had a working prototype (model) of the new camera. After briefly considering names like "Podak," Edwin decided to call it the Polaroid Land Camera Model 95.

Making a camera that instantly developed its own film was a tremendous achievement, but it was only part of the challenge. Both the camera and the film were extremely delicate. They had to be carefully manufactured. All of the elements had to work together exactly in order for the camera to function. After much searching, Edwin selected an appliance manufacturer to make the mechanical parts for Model 95. He asked Kodak to make the film. But another year of tests and adjustments were necessary before Edwin was satisfied that they had a camera reliable enough to sell.

Another problem that Edwin encountered was that no one at Polaroid had any experience in sales. In the past, Polaroid had sold to other manufacturers like Kodak and American Optical. Polaroid did not have people to sell, market, or advertise its product. For the new camera to succeed, Polaroid would have to create new departments.

As in the past, Edwin got the best people he could find for the jobs. He hired J. Harold Booth as executive vice-president and general manager for sales and marketing and Robert Casselman as sales manager.

"Polaroid" Becomes a Household Word

On February 21, 1947, Edwin unveiled his secret project. He chose the annual meeting of the Optical Society of America to reveal his new invention. Normally, scientific societies do not attract a lot of attention, but Edwin promised a spectacular surprise, so a great many reporters attended the meeting.

Edwin first unveiled his magical new camera in the late 1940s.

With his customary dramatic flair, Edwin demonstrated his camera before the crowd of scientists and journalists. No one in the room was prepared when the rectangle that emerged from the camera was peeled open to reveal a finished picture!

The audience was overjoyed. Reporters and photographers began crowding around Edwin, asking questions and taking pictures. Almost overnight the name *Polaroid* became a household word. People wanted to see the new camera that turned out instant pictures.

CHAPTER FOUR

ACCEPTING EVERY CHALLENGE

*Even in failure, Edwin remained true to his vision,
courageously pursuing his ideas and dreams.*

*P*olaroid announced that the new camera would be available by Christmas of 1948. This was another risky step. Although Edwin knew that his revolutionary product would work, he was still a little nervous about its production and distribution. Edwin now had sales and marketing people to bring his product to the American people, but he still worried that not enough cameras could be manufactured in time. He wanted each camera to meet rigid design specifications. With the cutbacks Polaroid suffered after the war, it couldn't afford to have faulty products

or many unsold cameras.

Fewer than 60 Model 95 cameras were ready by Thanksgiving of 1948. Because of the limited quantity, the sales people decided to sell the camera in only one store. Jordan Marsh in Boston, Massachusetts, was considered to be one of the countries finest department stores. Booth and Casselman agreed that Jordan Marsh was the right store in which to sell the first Polaroid Land Cameras.

Ever since that day in New Mexico, in fact ever since he was a boy, Edwin Land had

The Polaroid Land Camera Model 95 was first available to the public in Jordan Marsh stores at the end of 1948.

special feelings about photographs. More than anything else, he wanted to create a camera that would make it possible for anyone to take good pictures. With instant photography, you know right away if your picture hasn't come out or if you didn't get the shot you wanted. For the first time in photographic history, Edwin's instant camera made it possible to learn from mistakes immediately.

This meant that anyone, young or old, could become a photographer. If Edwin had sold his camera at camera stores instead of at Jordan Marsh, the salespeople there would probably have scared away ordinary people with all their talk about a camera's technical features. Edwin wanted to create a new market—people who in the past had been afraid of taking pictures or frustrated by their failures to take good ones.

To help make photography more inviting, Edwin also simplified the way the camera worked. He invented a new system for the adjustment of light settings that is still used in many cameras today. He also made the lens settings easier to use.

One of the most interesting things about the first Polaroid was that the pictures came out in sepia tones. Different from black-and-white photographs, sepia film gives Polaroid pictures a distinctive, timeless look in rich, reddish browns.

Edwin demonstrates the speed of his new camera to the president of the Photographic Society of America, Charles Phelps, in 1948.

Successful Marketing

To encourage people to take pictures, Polaroid offered a free roll of film to anyone who sent in the camera warranty. The company also set up a special phone number so people could ask questions about the film or the camera. This was another marketing strategy that has since been copied by many companies.

All these improvements contributed to making the Polaroid Land Camera one of the great marketing successes of the twentieth century. In the first year, Polaroid recorded sales totaling $5 million. It is estimated that in the first five years more than 200 million Polaroid pictures were taken. And just eight years after the camera went on sale, a million Polaroid cameras had been sold.

Perhaps because Edwin invented a camera designed for everyday use by ordinary people, some professional photographers and critics dismissed the new camera as an expensive toy. Serious photographers, they said, used only black-and-white prints.

Making Constant Improvements

Despite these objections, it was clear that Edwin had created a product that America needed and wanted. As the success of his camera spread, Edwin could have relaxed and collected money. But Edwin continued to work to improve his camera. Every few years, Polaroid offered something new. In 1950, it introduced black-and-white film. It also increased the size of the photographic image so that Polaroid pictures would be more suitable for professional photographers. Soon, even world-famous photographers were experimenting with Polaroids.

Polaroid invented new plastic materials to keep prints from fading. In 1955, the company also introduced faster-developing film. And in 1953, it began working on a way to produce color pictures. This was more complicated than producing black-and-white pictures because three different solutions had to interact on the film. It was difficult enough to do this in a darkroom, where three separate chemical baths were used, let alone in the back of a camera, where it would have to take place all at once.

Edwin and his researchers worked for 10 years to solve the problem of color film. The process was painstaking and expensive, and it required much experimentation. Edwin could have easily accepted the success of his first camera and been content, but he was too fascinated by the challenge.

The early Polaroids were expensive. For Edwin to fully realize his dream of making instant photography available to everyone, he had to make his camera more affordable. In 1965 Edwin came out with an inexpensive Swinger model.

Edwin's final version of the Polaroid was the SX-70, which came out in 1972. It was fittingly named, since this was the name of the secret file that Edwin had begun back in 1943. As in the past, the SX-70 showed Edwin's real willingness to take risks.

All the earlier Polaroids had been manufactured by companies working as subcontractors. But Edwin wanted Polaroid to make the SX-70. This required a huge investment, but it was the only way Edwin could control the process.

Edwin's work in the fields of optics, photography, and medicine has affected and improved the lives of people all over the world.

Edwin's Contributions to Society

Just as Edwin had tried to find ways to use polarizing sheets in everyday life, his breakthroughs in instant development and related technology now stimulated him to find other uses for instant photography. Using Polaroids for aerial photography, real-estate listing, and personal identification followed naturally.

And, just as Edwin had worked to develop a quinine substitute to fight malaria during World War II, he once again turned his talent and energy to aid in medical research. Edwin's company started making a special X-ray film that dramatically helped doctors identify internal injuries. It also developed a microscope that captured ultraviolet images on film. This new microscope allowed doctors and researchers to see color images of objects that were too small to be seen in normal light. In addition, Polaroid used its film in radiation badges. The badges could instantly indicate how much radiation a person had been exposed to.

In the fifties and sixties, the Polaroid Corporation rapidly grew to be one of the most successful firms in America. Land cameras represented the largest share of this growth, but Edwin's most useful contributions, such as glare-free street lights and stop signs and better instruments in hospitals and laboratories, were the ones most people didn't even realize he had made.

Disappointments Too

Many of Edwin's ideas never worked out in the way he had originally envisioned. Polaroid spent a great deal of time and money creating its own versions of photocopiers and color televisions. But these never really got off the ground. Edwin had also had high expectations for three-dimensional and Polaroid movies. Perhaps Edwin felt that these were his biggest disappointments and failures.

While he was developing the Polaroid Land camera, Edwin was also continuing work on creating three-dimensional images. This was the Vectograph project that he had developed for pilots during the war. Edwin thought that the same technology could be adapted for motion pictures. Polaroid spent millions of dollars on research and eventually succeeded in making 3-D movies possible.

The early films used two projectors that ran in sync. When moviegoers wore red and green plastic lenses, the overlapping images created the illusion of depth. Spears or knives seemed to fly off the screen toward the audience. For a time in the 1950s, 3-D seemed promising. Polaroid sold about 5 million pairs of the special glasses a year. For some reason, however, filmmakers never took full advantage of the possibilities. The 3-D films like *Bwana Devil* and *House of Wax* were not very good, and interest in 3-D soon faded. Most recently, 3-D was used in the final *Nightmare on Elm Street*, but such use is still rare.

Despite flaws, the educational and scientific advances in 3-D imagery are important. Today people use 3-D to test perception and to re-create terrain features on maps.

Edwin's interest in movies also led to another disappointment—the Polavision movie
system. Introduced in 1977, Polavision was a
movie camera with an instant-developing-
color-film cartridge. A movie, which lasted
fewer than three minutes, could be played
back on a viewer.

Had Polavision arrived earlier, it might
have done well. Unfortunately, however, it
came on the scene at about the same time as
Charles Ginsburg and his new video recorders,
which made longer, reusable picture and
sound recordings that could be played on
televisions. By 1979, Polaroid was forced to
abandon the Polavision dream.

Even in failure, Edwin remained true to his
vision, pursuing his ideas and dreams.

Edwin shows off his new Polavision camera at a press conference in 1977.

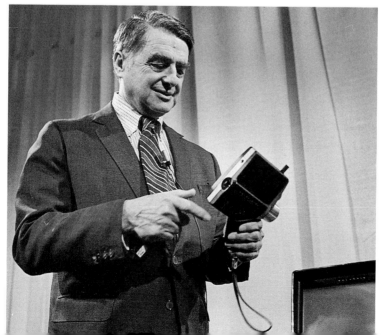

THE LATER YEARS

The list of his awards would fill many pages.

*A*s Polaroid's success increased, Edwin became one of the richest men in America. Wealth can be very isolating for some people, but this wasn't the case with Edwin. He continued to live in a modest home near his lab and walked to work every day. Although he enjoyed playing tennis, most of his socializing was among people with whom he shared a work connection.

Serving His Community

As he grew older, Edwin found a variety of ways to serve his community. He was an adviser to Presidents Eisenhower, Kennedy, Johnson, and Nixon. He remained active in scientific societies like the Optical Society of

Opposite: In 1980, Edwin stepped down as Polaroid's chairman. As an affectionate gesture, the company presented its founder with two small puppies.

Edwin and Vladimir Zworykin, inventor of the television, were inducted into the Inventors Hall of Fame on February 6, 1977.

America and the American Philosophical Society. He served as president of the American Academy of Arts and Sciences from 1951-1953.

Beginning in 1949 and continuing until his death in 1991, Edwin lectured at Boston-area colleges, most notably at Harvard and the Massachusetts Institute of Technology. He was often a visiting professor of physics, but he also taught courses in psychology.

As his interest in teaching grew, he became a generous contributor to higher education. He was a trustee of the Ford Foundation and a devoted member of the Carnegie Commission on Educational Television. To help familiarize students with the work of famous professors, Edwin created audio-visual presentations that simulated actual lectures. The presentations were so detailed that they even included the kinds of notes the professors may have written on their blackboards.

Research

Edwin also used his teaching as a springboard for developing his ideas about optics. Perhaps his most important contribution in this area was the Land Effect.

Edwin demonstrated that the human eye and brain play an important role in the way we see color. When he projected photographs on

Edwin sits with his successor and longtime colleague, William J. McCune.

a screen, using red and green filters, Edwin was able to fool viewers into believing that black-and-white photographs were in color. From this he concluded that the human eye constructs color out of three ranges of light wavelengths and that color is the result of the outside world acting upon the human eye. Edwin's work on optics is still not fully appreciated and remains an area for future study. Perhaps centuries after instant photography has been forgotten, optics will be the area for which Edwin Land is best remembered.

Retirement

In the 1970s, Edwin began to cut back on his work schedule. Finally, in 1975, he retired from the daily management of his company, making his longtime assistant, William McCune, president. Edwin, however, did remain as an adviser. He continued to work actively for more opportunities for women and minorities at Polaroid. And he continued to promote communication between workers and management. In the mid-seventies, he resigned from much of his committee work, but was still active in university programs.

The list of his awards, which includes the National Medal of Science and the President's Medal of Freedom, would fill many pages— few American scientists have done so much.

Edwin addresses stockholders at a 1982 meeting of the Polaroid Corporation.

In his later years, Edwin spent time with his wife and two daughters, Jennifer (Jeffie) and Valerie. He lectured occasionally and continued to develop his ideas about optics. Apart from tennis, Edwin's only other well-known outside interest was music.

On March 1, 1991, at the age of 81, Edwin Land died. During his long life, Edwin had seen nearly all his dreams come true. He was one of those rare individuals who lived life almost entirely on his own terms and whose life greatly affected all around him.

Glossary

fix To make a photographic image permanent by placing the negative in a solution.

molecule The smallest particle of a substance that retains all the properties of the substance.

optics The study of vision and light.

patent Government permission that allows a person to exclusively make, use, or sell an invention for a certain period of time.

polarizer A device that causes rays of light to exhibit different properties.

prototype An original model on which something is patterned.

radiation The process in which energy from one body is transmitted through a medium or space and then absorbed by another body.

silver haline A light-sensitive substance used to treat plastic film in a camera.

For Further Reading

Cumming, David. *Photography.* Milwaukee, WI: Raintree Steck-Vaughn, 1990.

Graham, Ian. *Cameras.* New York: Franklin Watts, 1991.

Jervis, Alastair. *Camera Technology.* New York: Franklin Watts, 1991.

Steffens, Bradley. *Photography: Preserving the Past.* San Diego, CA: Lucent Books, 1991.

Turvey, Peter. *Inventions: Inventors & Ingenious Ideas.* New York: Franklin Watts, 1992.

Index

Photo Credits:
Cover: Courtesy of Polaroid Corporate Archives.
P. 4: Gamma Liaison; p. 19, 29, 31: courtesy of Polaroid Corporate Archives; pp. 33, 36, 39, 43, 45: AP/Wide World Photos; pp. 40, 42: UPI/Bettmann.

Illustrations by Norman Merritt.

Special thanks to Nasrin Rohani, curator, Polaroid Corporate Archives.